LITTLE DREAMS

OF

LOVE

Illustrations by Julia Glynn Smith

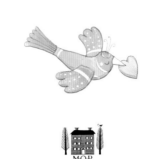

MQP

CONFETTI MOMENTS

how wild and
wonderful being
carried away
by you

you and me...

magic together

no matter where...

together with you

CONFETTI MOMENT

★ I ★

you're the one honeybee for me

love multiplied

midnight in the silver-soft garden

is every night with you

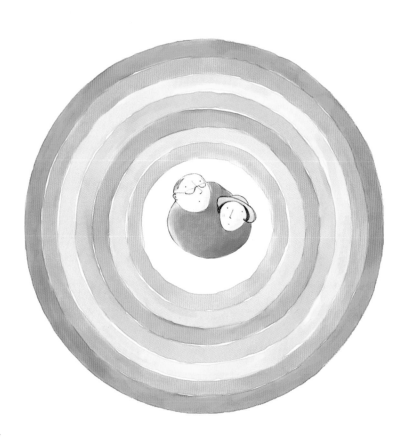

you and me

perfect happiness

and no end to

the rainbow

together ...
into the sunset

CONFETTI MOMENT
★ 2 ★

2
♥

How sweet
it is . . .

2

with you

anything is possible

the thought of you

makes me cartwheel

and somersault

all the way

to your place

I could dance

in the rain or sun

on Mars or on Venus

just thinking

of you

CONFETTI MOMENT

★ 3 ★

you send me over the
moon and happily
beyond reason

your love takes me
to the top of world

with you, I'm on cloud nine

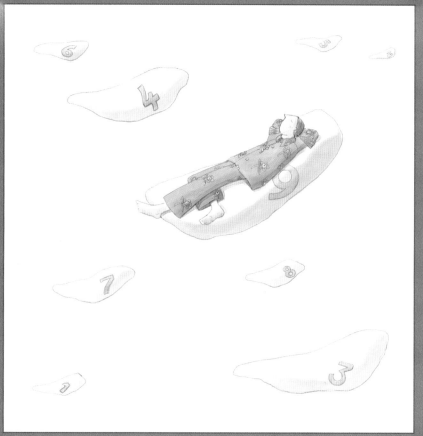

you make me feel like

singing out loud

Confetti Moment

★ 4 ★

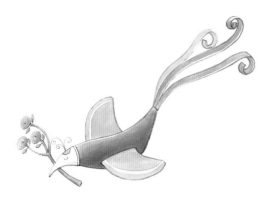

I bring you

my hopes

my dreams

and yes

my love

two lovebirds

two hearts

one promise

let me catch your bad dreams

CONFETTI MOMENT

★ 5 ★

breakfast in bed?

your wish is my command

I love it when

you keep me warm

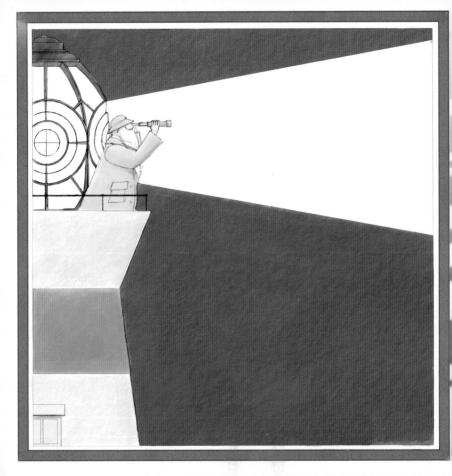

you always look out for me

take me away from it all

. . . my hero

CONFETTI MOMENT
★ 6 ★

4
♥

Without
you . . .

♠
4

no you

no love

no you

no heart

without you

I'm a party

waiting to happen

I can't face a day
without you

CONFETTI MOMENT

★ 7 ★

the *bed's* too big
without you

until you return

the minutes are light-years

and the world is

upside down

without you ...

totally blue

without you

the stars disappear

and even the moon is

all alone

when you're not
around...
there's a dark cloud
everywhere

C O N F E T T I   M O M E N T

★ 8 ★

...a remarkable
force of nature

...as deep as
the old village well

together we are timeless

CONFETTI MOMENT

★ 9 ★

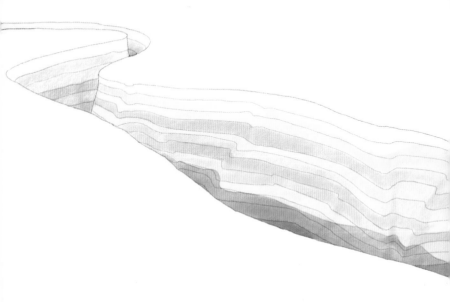

...another wonder

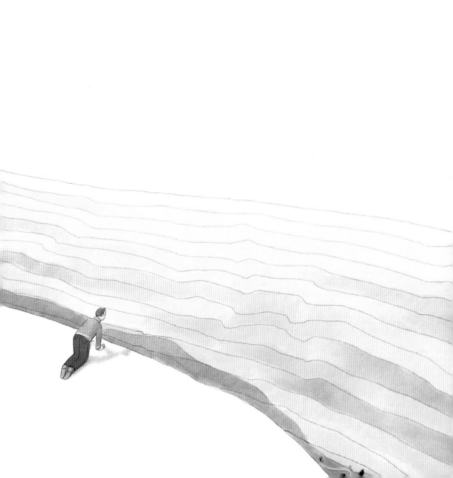

our love unfurls

like a ribbon

of moonlight

...a big bear hug

midnight skies

starlight sighs

and you

CONFETTI MOMENT

★ 10 ★

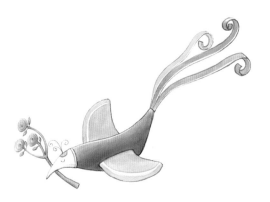

Julia Glynn Smith worked as an architect and designer before illustrating her first book. She lives in Islington, London, but is never happier than when stepping out with a new map in hand and new places to discover.

Published by MQ Publications Limited
254–258 Goswell Road, London EC1V 7RL
Tel: 020 7490 7732 / Fax: 020 7253 7358
e-mail: mqp@btinternet.com

Copyright © MQ Publications Limited 2000
Illustrations © Julia Glynn Smith 2000
Text © Lulu Colebrooke 2000

ISBN: 1-84072-076-X

1 3 5 7 9 0 8 6 4 2

Printed and bound in China